LYNNE GOLDSTEIN

THE GREAT MAHELE

KAMEHAMEHA III

(From a daguerreotype, courtesy Bernice P. Bishop Museum)

THE GREAT MAHELE

Hawaii's Land Division of 1848

Jon J. Chinen

THE UNIVERSITY PRESS OF HAWAII

First printing 1958
Second printing 1966
Third printing 1974
Fourth printing 1978

Copyright © 1958 by University of Hawaii Press
  (since July 1971 The University Press of Hawaii)
All rights reserved
Library of Congress Catalog Card Number 57-14473
ISBN 0-87022-125-6
Manufactured in the United States of America

To my wife, Winifred

PREFACE

The most important event in the reformation of the land system in Hawaii was *The Great Mahele* of 1848. This event separated and defined the undivided land interests of King Kamehameha III and the high-ranking chiefs and *konohikis*, and led to the end of the feudal system that existed in the Islands. However, *The Great Mahele* is still surrounded by confusion and misunderstanding.

In an attempt to understand *The Great Mahele* and its effect, I have studied thoroughly the events that preceded this momentous undertaking, the acts of King Kamehameha III and the high chiefs and *konohikis*, recorded as *The Great Mahele*, and the events that immediately followed. The Privy Council Records, the Journals of the Legislature, the records at the Office of Commissioner of Public Lands, and all the cases reported in the *Hawaii Reports* have been carefully analyzed. This book is the result of the research.

It is hoped that the materials in this book will be of aid to the reader in understanding and appreciating *The Great Mahele* of 1848.

Jon J. Chinen

Honolulu
1957

	Page
1. Ancient Land System	*1*
Map of Oahu, showing districts	*2*
2. The Land Commission	*8*
Facsimile of Land Commission Award	*10-11*
3. The Great Mahele	*15*
Facsimile of title page of The Mahele Book	*17*
Facsimile of pages from The Mahele Book	*18-19*
Facsimile of Royal Patent	*22*
4. Crown and Government Lands	*26*
Facsimile of Royal Patent (Grant)	*28*
5. Kuleana Lands	*29*
Bibliography	*33*

I. ANCIENT LAND SYSTEM

The date of man's first arrival in the Hawaiian Islands is not known. But by 1778, when Captain James Cook discovered the islands and made them known to the Western world as the Sandwich Islands, they were already well settled by a population of over 200,000 bronze-skinned Hawaiians.

Their lives having been closely associated from ancient times with the soil, the Hawaiians took great interest in the lands on which they lived and from which they derived their livelihood. For purposes of easier control and management, the Hawaiians divided all the lands within the Islands into a number of divisions, gave each division a separate name, and defined its boundaries to the best of their ability. Certain persons were trained to retain the knowledge of these divisions, and such knowledge was carefully passed on from generation to generation.[1]

To a large extent, the Hawaiians made the divisions of the lands along rational lines, following a mountain ridge, the bottom of a ravine, or the center of a stream or river. But oftentimes only the line of growth of a certain type of tree or grass marked a boundary; and sometimes only a stone determined the corner of a division.

1. Ralph S. Kuykendall, *The Hawaiian Kingdom, 1778-1854* (Honolulu: University of Hawaii, 1938); *Principles Adopted By The Board of Commissioners To Quiet Land Titles*, 1846, *Revised Laws of Hawaii, 1925*, vol. II, pp. 2120-2152; *Oni* v. *Meek*, 2 Hawaii 87 (1858); *In re Boundaries of Pulehunui*, 4 Hawaii 239 (1879); *Shipman* v. *Nawahi*, 5 Hawaii 571 (1886); *Harris* v. *Carter*, 6 Hawaii 195 (1877); *In re Boundaries of Kapoino*, 8 Hawaii 1 (1889); *Horner* v. *Kumuliilii*, 10 Hawaii 174 (1895); *In re Kakaako*, 30 Hawaii 666 (1928); *Territory* v. *Gay*, 31 Hawaii 376 (1930); *Territory* v. *Bishop Trust Company, Ltd.*, 41 Hawaii 358 (1956).

Map of Oahu, showing districts.

The largest unit or division of land was, naturally, the island. Each island was then divided into a number of districts called "*mokus*." These districts or *mokus* were geographical subdivisions only, and no administrators were assigned to them. The number of districts on each island varied, depending upon the size of the island. At the time of *The Great Mahele* of 1848, the Island of Oahu was divided into: Ewa, Kona, Koolauloa, Koolaupoko, Waialua, and Waianae. Since then, Kona has been renamed "Honolulu," and Wahiawa has been created from portions of Ewa, Waialua, and Waianae. These are important today as judicial districts. The unit next smaller to the district was the *kalana*. This, too, was a geographical subdivision only, and is not of much importance today.

A *moku* was divided for landholding purposes into units called "*ahupuaas*," each of which was ruled by either a chief or a *konohiki*. The ideal *ahupuaa* extended from the sea to the mountains, enabling the chief of the *ahupuaa* and his followers to obtain fish and seaweeds at the seashore, taro, bananas, and sweet potatoes from the lowlands, and forest products from the mountains. However, more often than not, an *ahupuaa* failed to extend to either the mountain or the seashore, being cut off from one or the other by the odd shapes of other *ahupuaas*. Although the *ahupuaa* has been called the "unit" of land in the Islands, it is not a measure of area as the acre is. While the acre contains a definite area, the *ahupuaas* vary in size. Though the smaller *ahupuaas* contain only a hundred acres of land, the larger ones contain more than 100,000 acres.

The unit next in size to the *ahupuaa* was called an "*ili*." While some *ahupuaas*, as the Ahupuaa of Waimanalo on Oahu, were without any *ili*,[2] several *ahupuaas* contained 30 or 40 *ilis*, each with its own name and carefully defined boundaries. Oftentimes, an *ili* consisted of several separate sections of land scattered over an island, one section along the seashore, a second in the lowlands, and another in the mountains. These separate sections were called "*leles*," from the verb *lele*, to jump.[3]

There were two principle types of *ili*, the *ili* of the *ahupuaa* and the *ili kupono*, often shortened to *ili ku*. The *ili* of the *ahupuaa* was a mere subdivision for the convenience

2. *Harris v. Carter, supra.*   3. *Horner v. Kumuliilii, supra.*

Ahupuaa of Kemau
Hamakua, Hawaii
L.C. Aw. 9971, Ap. 3
515 Acres

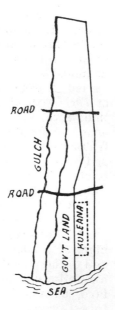

An ahupuaa (and kuleana within the ahupuaa) extending from the sea to the mountain, with one boundary along a gulch.

of the chief holding the *ahupuaa*, and the lesser chief, or *konohiki*, of such an *ili* of the *ahupuaa* was only an agent of the superior chief holding the *ahupuaa*. The Ili of Lihue in the Ahupuaa of Honouliuli was an *ili* of the *ahupuaa*.[4]

The *ili kupono* or *ili ku* was completely independent of the *ahupuaa* in which it was situated.[5] The chief of the *ili kupono* paid his tributes, not to the chief of the *ahupuaa* within which his *ili kupono* was situated, but directly to the king himself. Even when there were changes among the chiefs of the various *ahupuaas*, the chiefs of the *ili kuponos* within those *ahupuaas* were not affected. In some cases, the *ilis* within an *ahupuaa* absorbed the larger portion of the lands. On the Island of Hawaii, the Ili of Waikaloa and the Ili of Puukapu have included nine-tenths of the land in the Ahupuaa of Waimea.[6]

Some *ilis* do not appear to be in any *ahupuaa*, such as the *ilis* that were set apart as Fort Lands by the legislative Act of June 7, 1848. And there has never been an *ili* within an *ili*.[7]

4. *Harris* v. *Carter, supra.*
5. *Shipman* v. *Nawahi, supra; In re Kakaako, supra; Territory* v. *Gay, supra.*
6. *Harris* v. *Carter, supra.*   7. *In re Boundaries of Kapoino, supra.*

The arable portions of an *ili* were further subdivided into smaller tracts of land called *"moos"* or *"mooainas."* The *moo* was next in size to an *ili* and was set aside for purposes of cultivation only. The *moo* was then subdivided into lesser tracts called *"pauka,"* also set aside for purposes of cultivation.

The patches of land cultivated by the tenants or commoners for their chiefs or landlords were called *"koeles."* Later, because the tenants worked only on Fridays for their landlords, these patches became known as *Poalimas*, meaning Fridays. The smallest unit of land was called a *"kihapai,"* and was cultivated by a tenant-farmer for himself and his family.

At the time of Captain Cook's discovery of the Islands, the eight main islands were divided into several independent kingdoms. By right of conquest, each king was lord paramount and owner of all the lands within his jurisdiction. Immediately below the king were his warrior chiefs, and at the bottom were the tenant-commoners. After selecting the choicest lands for himself, the king allotted the remaining lands to the warrior chiefs who had rendered assistance in his conquest. These warrior chiefs, after retaining a portion for themselves, reallotted the remaining lands to their own followers and supporters. These reallotments of lands continued down to the lowest tenants, the common people. All these persons in possession of lands, superior and inferior, were considered as having certain rights in the products of the soil. Each individual was deemed entitled to a share of what he produced from the soil, gathered from the seashore, or collected from the mountains. These rights were not clearly defined, but were recognized and acknowledged by all.[8]

The distribution of lands were all on a revocable basis. What the superior gave, he was able to take away at pleasure. Because it was not considered just and right, dispossession did not occur too frequently. However, upon the death of a chief holding an *ahupuaa* or an *ili kupono,* numerous changes were made by the king, with the heirs of the decedent often ignored in favor of a new group of persons.

This ancient tenure was in nature feudal, although the

8. *Principles Adopted By The Board of Commissioners To Quiet Land Titles, supra; Keelikolani* v. *Robinson,* 2 Hawaii 522 (1862).

tenants were not serfs tied to the soil. They were allowed to move freely from the land of one chief to that of another. And the claims of the superior over the inferior were not for military services, but were for labor and products of the soil.

When King Kamehameha I brought all of the islands under his control at the beginning of the nineteenth century, he simply utilized the land system in existence.[9] After setting aside the lands he desired for his personal use and enjoyment, Kamehameha I divided the rest among his principal warrior chiefs for distribution to the lesser chiefs and, down the scale, to the tenant-commoners.

These allotments were still on a revocable basis. However, to a great extent, Kamehameha I permitted the heirs of a deceased chief to remain on the *ahupuaa* or *ili kupono* previously granted by him to the chief. The tenure was still nonmilitary, and the tenants were free to move from the land of one chief to that of another.

All persons in possession of land, from the superior chiefs down to the tenant-commoners, owed and paid to Kamehameha I not only a land tax, but also services which he called for at his discretion. In addition to the yearly taxes, they also paid a portion of the products of the land. And they owed obedience to the king at all times.

Upon the death of Kamehameha I on May 8, 1819, in accordance with his will his son Liholiho was recognized as King Kamehameha II. With the crown the new king inherited his father's absolute sovereign powers over the Islands. Kamehameha II made only a few changes in the distribution of lands, leaving the great majority of the lands with the chiefs who had been rewarded by his father. These sovereign powers descended with the crown to Kauikeaouli who became King Kamehameha III upon the death of his brother in England on July 14, 1824.[10]

When Kamehameha III ascended the throne, he found a large foreign population in the Islands. The fur and sandalwood trades and the whaling industry in the Pacific Ocean had brought to the Islands aggressive sailors, traders, and

9. *Principles Adopted By The Board of Commissioners To Quiet Land Titles, supra; In re Matters of Estate of His Majesty Kamehameha IV,* 2 Hawaii 715 (1864).

10. *In re Matters of Estate of His Majesty Kamehameha IV, supra; Kapiolani Estate* v. *Atcherly,* 21 Hawaii 441 (1913), 238 United States 119 (1915).

merchants. Many of them had been accustomed in their homeland to possessing lands in fee simple, and vigorously challenged the right of the king and the chiefs to dispossess them at will. Meanwhile, the missionaries who first came to the Islands in 1820 also strove to change the system of land tenure, partly to improve the status of the tenant-commoners and partly so they, too, could possess land in fee simple.

The vigorous actions of the foreigners in the Islands, often supported by the commanders of the warships of their homelands visiting at the time in Hawaiian waters, forced Kamehameha III and his chiefs to review their national policy. Their study led to the enactment of the Bill of Rights of 1839,[11] which was the beginning of a complete change in the government and in the land system in Hawaii.

In the Bill of Rights, often called the "Magna Charta of Hawaii," rights of the people were defined and protected. Part of the Bill of Rights reads, "Protection is hereby secured to the persons of all the people, together with their lands, their building lots and all their property, and nothing whatever shall be taken from any individual, except by express provision of the law." The Act further stated that the "landlord cannot causelessly dispossess his tenant," and it also defined what was sufficient cause.

The Bill of Rights was followed by the first constitution of the Hawaiian Kingdom, granted by King Kamehameha III on October 8, 1840.[12] This constitution changed the Hawaiian government from an absolute monarchy to a constitutional monarchy. Among other things, the constitution established a bicameral legislature consisting of a house of nobles and a representative body chosen by the common people. This representative body permitted the commoners to participate for the first time in their government. Another important feature was the creation of a supreme court, consisting of the king, the king's adviser known as the *kuhina-nui*, and four judges appointed by the representative body. A third important feature was the declaration

11. *In re Matters of Estate of His Majesty Kamehameha IV, supra; Kapiolani Estate* v. *Atcherly, supra; Principles Adopted By The Board of Commissioners To Quiet Land Titles, supra.*

12. *In re Matters of Estate of His Majesty Kamehameha IV, supra;* Lorrin A. Thurston, *The Fundamental Law of Hawaii* (Honolulu: The Hawaiian Gazette Company, Ltd., 1904), pp. 1-9.

that, though all the land belonged to King Kamehameha I, "it was not his own private property. It belonged to the chiefs and people in common, of whom Kamehameha I was the head, and had management of the landed property." This was the first formal acknowledgment by the king that the common people had some form of ownership in the land, aside from an interest in the products of the soil.

Under the constitution, the common people were still unable to acquire absolute ownership of the land which they cultivated and on which they lived. However, they were no longer subject to arbitrary removal by the king or his chiefs.

2. THE LAND COMMISSION

The first important step in the reformation of the system of land tenure in the Islands was the enactment of the statute of December 10, 1845, creating the Board of Commissioners To Quiet Land Titles, commonly referred to as the Land Commission.[1] The statute provided for a board of five commissioners to be appointed by King Kamehameha III "for the investigation and final ascertainment or rejection of all claims of private individuals, whether natives or foreigners, to any landed property acquired anterior to the passage of this Act." It stated that the awards of the Land Commission, unless appealed to the Supreme Court, "shall be binding upon the Minister of Interior and upon the applicant."

The Act required the Land Commission to publish in a newspaper a notice concerning its special powers, its place of meeting and its mode of procedure in the performance of its duties. It declared that all persons, natives and for-

1. *Knudsen* v. *Board of Education*, 8 Hawaii 60 (1890); *Kapiolani Estate* v. *Atcherly*, 21 Hawaii 441 (1913), 238 United States 119 (1915); *Bishop* v. *Kalua*, 36 Hawaii 164 (1942); *Revised Laws of Hawaii, 1925*, vol. II, pp. 2120-2152; *Laws of Hawaii, 1846*, p. 107; Lorrin A. Thurston. *The Fundamental Law of Hawaii* (Honolulu: The Hawaiian Gazette Company, Ltd., 1904), pp. 137-154. This statute was later re-enacted as Article IV of *An Act to Organize the Executive Department of the Hawaiian Islands*, April 27, 1846.

eigners, with claims to interests in lands were required to present their claims to the Land Commission within two years after such notice had been published. No exceptions were made in favor of infants.[2]

The Land Commission was required to render its decisions in accordance with the "principles established by the civil code of the kingdom in regard to prescription, occupancy, fixtures, native usages in regard to landed tenures, water privileges and rights of piscary, the rights of women, the rights of absentees, tenancy and subtenancy-- primogeniture and rights of adoption." The Land Commission had no authority to create any new interest in land; it was granted only the authority to determine the rights in land existing as of the date of the Act. Upon the confirmation of a claim and the issuance of an award by the Land Commission to a successful claimant, the statute authorized the minister of interior to issue a Royal Patent on the Award, upon payment of commutation to the government.

The first five members appointed to the Land Commission were William Richards, who was elected chairman by the other members, John Ricord, then the attorney general of the kingdom, Zorobabela Kaauwai, James Young Kaneohoa, and John Ii.[3] The Land Commission held its first meeting on February 11, 1846. After organizing, it started on its first task, the formulation of the principles to guide its decisions. After a thorough study of the history of the Hawaiian land system, the Land Commission issued a document entitled *Principles Adopted By the Board of Commissioners to Quiet Land Titles in Their Adjudication of Claims Presented to Them.*[4]

In the preface to its *Principles,* the Land Commission analyzed in detail the land system existing at the time in the Islands. It then declared that "there are but three classes of persons having vested rights in the land, 1st, the government (the king), 2nd, the landlord (the chief and the *konohiki*), and 3rd, the tenant." After declaring that, under another act of the legislature, aliens were prohibited

2. *Thurston* v. *Bishop,* 7 Hawaii 421 (1888); *Kapiolani Estate* v. *Atcherly, supra.*

3. *Principles Adopted By The Board of Commissioners To Quiet Land Titles, supra.*

4. These principles are fully set out in *Revised Laws of Hawaii, 1925,* vol. II, pp. 2120-2152.

Claim No. 133 William Browningburgh

This is a claim to a Land in Waikapu, Island of Maui, Known by the name of "Pohakoi."

From the evidence it appears that the claimant, owning in right of his Wife, a small land in Waikapu by the name of Pilipili, exchanged the same with Pupa-hehae in the Year A.D. 1832 for "Pohakoi"; the land now Claimed; and that he has Continued to occupy the same in peace down to the present time.

This title is made Clear by the first Rule of the Board; and we do therefore award to the aforesaid Claimant, William Browningburgh, a freehold title less than allodial; or in other words a Life Estate in said land; which he may Commute for a fee simple title as prescribed by law.

The Survey of the above awarded lands is as follows:—

"Notes of Survey of Pohakoii in Waikapu Maui"

"Commencing at S.E. corner of Wall enclosing the lot, joining Antonio Catalena's land, and Running N. 8° 30' W. 7 Ch. 6½ ft. along E. Wall to angle - thence N. 25° W. 9 ft. to N.E. Corner of this lot - thence S. 82° 15' W. 3 Ch. 60 ft. along N. Wall to angle - thence S. 37° W. 1 Ch. 19½ ft. along wall to angle - thence S. 23° 15' W. 39½ ft. along Wall to Wm. Humphreys land - Thence S. 4° W. 5 Ch. 17½ ft. along Wm. Humphreys to S.W. corner of this land - Thence S. 87° E. 1 Ch. 27½ ft. along A. Catalena's to angle of Wall. thence direct to place of Commencet. Including an area of.   Acres 5 92/100

Metcalf Surr.

Sep. 29. 1847.

Facsimile of Land Commission Award.

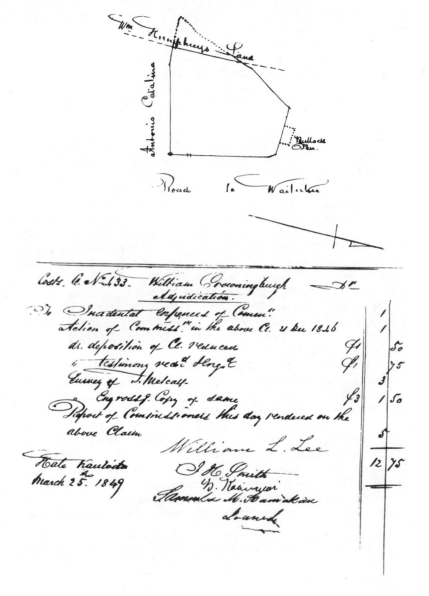

Costs. C. No 133. William Grooningburgh — Dr
                    Adjudication.

To Incidental Expences of Comm":
  Action of Comm"s in the above Ce. 21 Dec 1846   1
    dr. deposition of Ce. reduced $1   50
    ,, testimony read'd long'd $1   75
  Survey of J. Metcalf.   3
    ,, Engross'g Copy of same $3   1 50
  Report of Commissioners this day rendered on the
    above Claim   5

                William L. Lee
                                                          12 75
State Kauloa'u   J H Smith
March 25. 1849   H. Kaimanei
              Samuel M. Kamakau
                    Learned

from acquiring any allodial or fee simple estate in land, the Land Commission listed the seven principles that were to guide its decisions.

The first five principles outlined the nature of the inquiries that were to be made by the Land Commission in examining the various claims to land. The sixth covered the matter of commutation to the government and the seventh principle emphatically declared that anyone not filing a claim with the Land Commission on or before February 14, 1848[5] forfeited his interest in the land to the government. These principles were enacted into law by the approval thereof on October 26, 1846, by the legislative council.[6]

At the outset, the Land Commission was greatly handicapped in the performance of its duties. Since it was without the power and authority to separate the undivided interests of the king, the chiefs and *konohikis*, and the tenant-commoners in the lands until these undivided interests were defined and separated, the Land Commission was unable to render awards to the greater portions of the lands in the Islands. Thus, during the first few years after its creation, the Land Commission handled claims mainly for leasehold interests, with only a handful of natives filing claims for lands in fee simple.

It was after the completion of *The Great Mahele* of 1848,[7] followed by the passage of the Act of July 10, 1850,[8] authorizing the sale of lands in fee simple to resident aliens, and the passage of the Act of August 6, 1850,[9] authorizing the award of *kuleanas* to native tenants, that the Land Commission was able to truly distinguish itself. Subsequent to those events and until its dissolution in 1853, the Land Commission handled over 12,000 individual claims for lands. The awards issued by the Land Commission have been recorded in ten huge volumes, and the testimony on which the Land Commission rendered its decisions has

5. This date was extended from time to time by subsequent legislative enactments.

6. *Thurston* v. *Bishop, supra; Laws of Hawaii, 1847; Revised Laws of Hawaii, 1925*, vol. II, p. 2137.

7. *The Great Mahele* is covered in section 3.

8. *Laws of Hawaii, 1850*, p. 146; *Revised Laws of Hawaii, 1925*, vol. II, pp. 2233-2234.

9. This Act is covered in section 5.

been recorded in 50 lesser volumes. Both of these sets of volumes are today retained in the Office of the Commissioner of Public Lands.

The Land Commission was in effect a judicial court.[10] Upon receipt of a claim to a parcel of land, it set a definite date for a hearing. After studying the evidence presented, it then either confirmed or rejected a claim. The successful claimant was issued an award called "Land Commission Award," commonly abbreviated "L. C. Aw."

Except for appeals to the Supreme Court, the decisions of the Land Commission were final. And the Supreme Court of Hawaii has refused to go behind an award to inquire whether or not such an award had been obtained by fraud.[11]

The members of the Land Commission traveled to various parts of the different islands to hear the claims of the chiefs and people. Originally intended to exist for only two years, statutes were enacted from time to time extending the life of the Land Commission until its dissolution on March 31, 1855.

The awards issued by the Land Commission identified the nature of the title conferred, as being either fee simple or leasehold. And the awards issued during the first few years after the creation of the Land Commission also defined the boundaries of the lands confirmed, the surveys being made at the expense of the successful claimants.

Except for the government's right of commutation, a Land Commission Award gave complete title to the lands confirmed. The commutation was satisfied by the payment of cash or the return of land of equal value. The commutation was generally one third of the value of the unimproved land as of the date of the award.[12] However, the commuta-

10. *Dowsett* v. *Maukeala*, 10 Hawaii 166 (1895); *Kapiolani Estate* v. *Atcherly*, 21 Hawaii 447 (1913). However, the Land Commission did not decide on the question of a right of way, nor of fisheries, except incidentally to its other duties. *Jones* v. *Meek*, 2 Hawaii 9 (1857). *Bishop* v. *Mahiko*, 35 Hawaii 608 (1940).
11. *Kukiiahu* v. *Gill*, 1 Hawaii 54, 90 (1851); *Kekiekie* v. *Dennis*, 1 Hawaii 69 (1851); *Kalama* v. *Kekuanoa & Ii*, 2 Hawaii 202 (1857); *Bishop* v. *Namakaala & Kahinukawa*, 2 Hawaii 238 (1860); *Keelikolani* v. *Robinson*, 2 Hawaii 436, 522 (1862); *Kaai* v. *Mahuka*, 5 Hawaii 354 (1885); *In re Title of Pa Pelekane*, 21 Hawaii 175 (1912); *Territory* v. *Gay*, 26 Hawaii 382 (1922); *In re Kakaako*, 30 Hawaii 666 (1928).
12. On October 16, 1892, a statute was enacted setting the commutation to be paid by certain chiefs and *konohikis* at one third of the unimproved value of the land at the date of the *mahele*.

tion for house lots in Honolulu, Lahaina, and Hilo was set by the Privy Council at one fourth of the value of the unimproved land as of the date of the award.[13] Upon satisfaction of the commutation to the government, a Royal Patent upon the Award was issued by the minister of interior.

A Royal Patent issued upon a Land Commission Award did not confer or confirm title. It merely quitclaimed the government's interest in the land. It was evidence that the government's right to commutation had been extinguished. And all the presumptions have been held in favor of the validity of a patent.[14]

Even without a Royal Patent, the recipient of a Land Commission Award was fully able to protect his interests in the lands confirmed to him. The Act of August 10, 1854,[15] which provided for the dissolution of the Land Commission on March 31, 1855, emphatically stated that "a Land Commission Award shall furnish as good and sufficient a ground upon which to maintain an action for trespass, ejectment, and other real action, against any person or persons whatsoever, as if the claimant, his heirs or assigns, had received a Royal Patent for the same."

For many years there being no means of dispossessing the recipient of an award who failed to pay his commutation, a great number of persons made no effort to pay the commutation to the government. It was not until 1909 that a statute was enacted establishing a procedure for enforcing the payment for such commutation.[16] Only then did many chiefs fulfill their obligations to the government.

13. *Minister of Interior* v. *Papaikou Sugar Co.*, 8 Hawaii 125 (1890).

14. *Laanui* v. *Puohu*, 2 Hawaii 161 (1859); *Davis* v. *Brewer*, 3 Hawaii 270 (1871); 3 Hawaii 359 (1872); *Brunz* v. *Smith*, 3 Hawaii 783 (1877); *Greenwell* v. *Paris*, 6 Hawaii 315 (1882); *Mist* v. *Kawelo*, 11 Hawaii 587 (1898).

15. *Laws of Hawaii, 1854; Revised Laws of Hawaii, 1925*, vol. II, pp. 2146-2147.

16. *Laws of Hawaii, 1909*, chap. 90, sect. 1.

3. THE GREAT MAHELE

The most important event in the reformation of the land system in Hawaii was the separation and identification of the relative rights of the king, the chiefs, and the *konohikis*, in the lands within the Islands. This event led to the end of the feudal system in the kingdom.

In the preface to its *Principles* adopted in 1846, as a suggestion to an equitable distribution of lands within the Islands, the Land Commission had recommended the separation of equally valuable lands into three parts: one part to be retained by the king, one part to be set aside to the chiefs and *konohikis*, and the third part to be distributed to the tenants or common people. However, there was no action taken on the suggestion. Neither King Kamehameha III nor the chiefs were then ready for such a drastic departure from the old system.

It was not easy for Kamehameha III and the chiefs to arrive at an agreement for the distribution of the various undivided interests in the lands. The matter was seriously discussed for over a year in both the Legislative Assembly and the Privy Council.[1] Then, in December of 1847, the matter was brought to a final determination in the Privy Council. By then, the king and the chiefs realized that the economy of the Islands could not advance under the old feudal system of land tenure. After several days of discussion, on December 18, the Privy Council adopted a set of rules and created a committee to assist the king and the chiefs and the *konohikis* in separating and defining their various rights and interests in the lands within the kingdom.[2]

The first members appointed to the committee were John Young, G. P. Judd, J. Piikoi, and M. Kekuanaoa. The rules adopted as guides for the king and the chiefs were in substance as follows: (1) The king was to retain all of his private lands as his own individual property, subject only to the rights of tenants. (2) One third of the remaining lands was to be for the Hawaiian Government; one third for

---

1. For example: Journals of the Legislature, October 19, 22, 24, 30, 1846; *Privy Council Records*, vol. II, p. 308; vol. IV, p. 226.
2. *Privy Council Records*, vol. II, pp. 250-308.

the chiefs and *konohikis*; and one third to be set aside for the tenants, the actual possessors and cultivators of the soil. (3) The division between the chiefs and *konohikis* and their tenants under Rule 2 was to take place whenever any chief, *konohiki*, or tenant desired such a division, subject only to confirmation by the king in privy council. (4) The tenants of the king's private lands were entitled to a fee simple title to one third of the lands possessed and cultivated by them, which was to be set off for the tenants in fee simple, whenever the king or any of the tenants desired such a division. (5) The divisions prescribed in the foregoing rules were not to interfere with any lands that may have been granted in fee simple by the king or his predecessors. (6) The chiefs and *konohikis* were authorized to satisfy the commutation by either the setting aside of one third of their lands to the government or by the payment of one third of the unimproved value of their lands. (7) The lands of King Kamehameha III were to be recorded in the same book as all other allodial titles, and the only separate book was to be that listing the government lands. It was Kamehameha III who insisted upon the seventh rule, as a means of protecting his private lands in the event of an invasion of the Islands by a foreign power.

More than two hundred and forty of the highest ranking chiefs and *konohikis* in the kingdom joined Kamehameha III in this momentous task. The first *mahele*, or division, of lands was signed on January 27, 1848, by Kamehameha III and Princess Victoria Kamamalu by her guardians Mataio Kekuanaoa and Ioane Ii; the last *mahele* was signed by the king and E. Enoka on March 7, 1848.[3]

Each *mahele*, or division, was in effect a quitclaim agreement between the king and a chief or a *konohiki* with reference to the lands in which they both claimed interests. In each *mahele*, after certain lands were listed as belonging to the king, the chief or the *konohiki* who participated in that particular *mahele* signed an agreement in the following form: "I hereby agree that this division is good. The lands above written are for the King. I have no more rights therein." The remaining lands were set aside for the chief

---

3. The Mahele Book, Office of the Commissioner of Public Lands, Territory of Hawaii; *Harris* v. *Carter*, 6 Hawaii 195 (1877); *In re Kakaako*, 30 Hawaii 666 (1928).

Buke Kakau Paa

no ka mahele aina

i Hooholoia

iwaena o

Kamehameha III

a me

Na Lii

a me

Na Konohiki ana

Hale Alii Honolulu

Ianuari

1848.

Facsimile of title page of The Mahele Book.

Ko Kamehameha III.

Ka aina	ahupuaa	Kalana	Mokupuni
Ko Pakui	Li no Kaneohe	Koolau Poko	Oahu

Ke ae aku nei au i keia mahele, ua maikai. No ka Moi ka 1/2 aina i kakauia maluna. aohe ou kuleana maloko.

no Luu

Hale Alii
Feburuari 14, 1848

Ko Kamehameha III.

Ka aina	ahupuaa	Kalana	Mokupuni
Kuoa	Li no Kaneohe	Koolau Poko	Oahu

Ke ae aku nei au i keia mahele, ua maikai. No ka Moi ka aina i kakauia maluna. aohe ou kuleana maloko.

no Hoohano Kaao

Hale Alii
11 Feb 1848

Ko Kamehameha III.

aina	ahupuaa	Kalana	Mokupuni
1/2 Lauka		Hamakua	Hawaii

Ke ae aku nei au i keia mahele, ua maikai. No ka Moi ka Moi ka 1/2 aina i kakau ia maluna. aohe ou kuleana maloko.

moluae

Hale Alii
1 Feb 1848

Ko Kamehameha III.

Ka aina	ahupuaa	Kalana	Mokupuni
Hopeolaa	Lii . Halawa	Kohala	Hawii

Ke ae aku nei au i keia mahele, ua maikai. No ka Moi ka aina i kakauia maluna: aohe ou kuleana maloko.

E Kaleionehu

Hale Alii
11 Feb. 1848

No Keo Luu.

ʻaina	ahupuaa	Kalana	Mokupuni
J. Pukui	Ili no Kaueohea	Koolau Poko	Oahu

He ae aku nei au i keia mahele, ua maikai.
No Keo Luu ka po aina i kakauia maluna: ua ae ia
kuu hiki ke lawe aku iwaua o ka Berberena Aloha a.

Kamehameha

Hale alii:
Feberuari 10, 1848

Ko Kahoohanohano.

Ka aina	ahupuaa	Kalana	Mokupuni
maoli	Ili no Waiohole	Koolau Poko	Oahu

He ae aku nei au i keia mahele, ua maikai. No Kahoohanohano ka aina i kakauia maluna: ua ae ia kuu e hiki ke lawe aku iwaua ka
Po Hoona Aukana

Kamehameha

Hale Alii
11 ... 1848

Ko Puuloa.

aina	ahupuaa	Kalana	Mokupuni
1o Kaaehia		Hamakua	Hawaii

He ae aku nei au i keia mahele, ua maikai. No
Maluae ka po aina i kakauia maluna: ua ae ia 'k
e hiki ke lawe aku iwaua o ka Po Hoona Aukana.

Kamehameha

Hale alii
14, Febe. 1848

Ko Kalaionehu.

Ka aina	ahupuaa	Kalana	Mokupuni
Alaeanui	Ili Kalauao	Ewa	Oahu

He ae aku nei au i keia mahele, ua maik.
No Kalaionehu ka aina i kakau ia maluna: ua
ae ia 'ku e hiki ke lawe aku iwaua o ka Po   ma
Aukana

Kamehameha

Hale alii
1o, Febe. 1848

or *konohiki* who participated in the *mahele* and the king signed an agreement in the following form: "I hereby agree that this division is good. The lands above written are for [name of chief or *konohiki*]: consent is given to take it before the Board of Commissioners To Quiet Land Titles."[4] These lands set aside for the chiefs and *konohikis* became known as "*konohiki* lands."

The individual divisions, or *maheles*, were all recorded in a huge book called the "Mahele Book," and these divisions have been called "*The Mahele*" or "*The Great Mahele.*" In the Mahele Book, the lands reserved for the king have been listed on the left side and those quitclaimed to the chiefs and *konohikis* on the right. Though these individual divisions were performed on separate days over a period of about a month and a half, they have been considered as one transaction.[5]

Because of the lack of surveyors in the Islands during this period, the *mahele* was made without any survey. All the lands being divided according to their ancient names and boundaries, there was no uniformity in the divisions of the lands. While some chiefs had quitclaimed to them *ahupuaas* covering over a hundred thousand acres of land extending from the sea up into the mountains, others had quitclaimed to them *ili kuponos* covering a few hundred acres of land situated only along the seashore or only in the mountains.

Ili kuponos were the only *ilis* recognized in *The Mahele*. Because the *ilis* of the *ahupuaa* went with the *ahupuaas* in which they were situated, after *The Mahele*, they were no longer distinguished. Kamehameha III reserved for himself both *ahupuaas* and *ili kuponos*. In some instances, as the Ahupuaa of Wailuku on the Island of Maui, while Kamehameha III reserved the *ahupuaa*, the *ilis* therein were quitclaimed to different *konohikis*.[6]

The Mahele itself did not convey any title to land. The high chiefs and the lesser *konohikis* who participated in *The Mahele* and who were named in the Mahele Book were required to present their claims before the Land Commission and to receive awards for the lands quitclaimed to them by Kamehameha III. Until an award for these lands

4. The Mahele Book, *supra; Harris* v. *Carter, supra.*
5. *Harris* v. *Carter, supra.*   6. *Harris* v. *Carter, supra.*

was issued by the Land Commission, title to such lands remained with the government.[7]

Since the *mahele*, or division, had been completed without survey, on June 19, 1852,[8] the legislature authorized the *konohikis* who participated in *The Mahele* to obtain awards to their lands by their ancient names, with the understanding that the ancient boundaries were to control until a survey could be made. This act, however, did not apply to *ahupuaas* or *ili kuponos* which had to be divided between the king and a *konohiki*, or between two *konohikis*, or between the government and a *konohiki*.

Even after receiving a Land Commission Award for a tract of land, the recipient did not acquire a free and clear title. He was still required to pay commutation to the government, in cash or by the surrender of equally valuable lands. This commutation was originally set at one third of the value of the unimproved land as of the date of the award.[9] However, on December 16, 1892, in an act passed for the relief of certain *konohikis*, it was declared that "the Government shall receive one-third of the unimproved value of such lands at the date of such *mahele*."[10] Upon payment of the commutation, the minister of interior issued to the chief or *konohiki* a Royal Patent upon the award.[11]

Because many who had participated in *The Mahele* had failed to file their claims for their lands with the Land Commission within the time allowed by law, on August 10, 1854,[12] these persons were granted an extension of time. After the expiration of the Land Commission on March 31, 1855, it was learned that there were many *konohikis* who

7. *Kanaina* v. *Long*, 3 Hawaii 335 (1872); *Kahoomana* v. *Moehonua*, 3 Hawaii 635 (1875); *Pedro* v. *Farr*, 4 Hawaii 461 (1883); *Kenoa* v. *Meek*, 6 Hawaii 63 (1871); *Harris* v. *Carter*, *supra*; *Thurston* v. *Bishop*, 7 Hawaii 438 (1888); *Rose* v. *Yoshimura*, 11 Hawaii 30 (1897); *Atcherly* v. *Lewers & Cooke*, 18 Hawaii 639 (1908), 222 United States 285 (1911); *In re Title of Pa Pelekane*, 21 Hawaii 175 (1912); *Territory* v. *Hutchinson Sugar Plantation Co.*, 272 Fed. 856 (1921); *Territory* v. *Gay*, 26 Hawaii 382 (1922); *In re Austin (Land Title, Waimalu)*, 33 Hawaii 832 (1936).

8. *Laws of Hawaii, 1852; Revised Laws of Hawaii, 1925*, vol. II, p. 2144.

9. *Thurston* v. *Bishop*, *supra*; *Minister of Interior* v. *Papaikou Sugar Co.*, 8 Hawaii 125 (1890).

10. Act of December 16, 1892; *Revised Laws of Hawaii, 1925*, vol. II, pp. 2151-2152.

11. *Laanui* v. *Puohu*, 2 Hawaii 161 (1859).

12. *Laws of Hawaii, 1854*, p. 25; *Revised Laws of Hawaii, 1925*, vol. II, p. 2147.

NO. *1612*

ROYAL PATENT,
UPON CONFIRMATION OF THE LAND COMMISSION.

Whereas, the Board of Commissioners to Quiet Land Titles have by their decision awarded unto *Akoni* *claim N° 2944, B.* an estate of **Freehold** less than Allodial, in and to the land hereafter described, and whereas *the said Akoni has commuted the title, as awarded for a Fee-Simple title by the payment of six dollars into the Royal Exchequer;*

Therefore, Kamehameha, by the grace of God, King of the Hawaiian Islands, by this Royal Patent, makes known unto all men, that he has, for himself and his successors in office, this day granted and given absolutely, in **Fee Simple,** unto *Akoni*

all that certain piece of land situate at *Kapuukolo Honolulu* in the Island of *Oahu* , and described as follows :

Commencing at the North angle & running
S. 57° E. 34 9/12 feet along Kaluu Pakohana
S. 44° W. 47 " " Capt Maughan's land
N. 40° W. 42 1/2 " " Kahanaike
N. 61° E. 40/12 " " O. B. Marini to the place of beginning

containing *0.073* acres, more or less ; excepting and reserving to the Hawaiian Government all mineral or metalic mines of every description.

To have and to hold the above granted land in **Fee Simple** unto the said *Akoni his* heirs and assigns forever, subject to the taxes to be from time to time imposed by the Legislative Council equally upon all landed property held in Fee Simple.

In witness whereof I have hereunto set my hand and caused the Great Seal of the Hawaiian Islands to be affixed, this *thirtieth* day of *August* 1853

Kamehameha

Kaui Ana

had not obtained awards to their lands. For their relief, on August 24, 1860,[13] the legislature passed an act which authorized the *konohikis* whose names appeared in the Mahele Book of 1848 to present their claims and obtain awards to their lands from the minister of interior. The *konohikis* were given until June 30, 1862, to present their claims. The *mahele* awards issued under this 1860 statute were of equal weight to those awards that had been issued by the Land Commission.[14] The act authorized the lands awarded to the *konohikis* to be described by survey or by their ancient boundaries pursuant to the Act of June 19, 1852.

To settle the question of the boundaries of these *ahupuaas* and *ili kuponos* that had been awarded by their ancient names without survey, the legislature on August 23, 1862, created the Commissioner of Boundaries.[15] All persons who had received awards for their lands by names only were required to appear before the Commissioners to have their boundaries determined and identified. Under this statute, the minister of interior was forbidden to issue any patent in confirmation of an award without the boundaries of the land being defined by the Boundary Commissioners.

Where *ahupuaas* or *ili kuponos* have been awarded by name only, such awards have been determined to include everything within the ancient boundaries, except for the tracts of land previously detached from the *ahupuaa* or ili *kupono*.[16] Where the tracts of land have been awarded by metes and bounds, such awards have been determined to include all the lands within the metes and bounds, excepting only that which was expressly reserved.[17]

13. *Laws of Hawaii, 1860*, p. 27; *Revised Laws of Hawaii, 1925*, vol. II, p. 2148.

14. *Territory* v. *Gay*, 26 Hawaii 382 (1922).

15. *Laws of Hawaii, 1862*, p. 27; *Board of Education* v. *Bailey*, 3 Hawaii 702 (1876); *Boundaries of Kapoino*, 8 Hawaii 1 (1889); *In re Title of Kioloku*, 25 Hawaii 357 (1920).

16. *Keelikolani* v. *Robinson*, 2 Hawaii 522 (1862); *Kanaina* v. *Long, supra; In re Boundaries of Pulekunui*, 4 Hawaii 239 (1879); *Cornwell* v. *Board of Education*, 4 Hawaii 540 (1882); *Harris* v. *Carter, supra; Territory* v. *Liliuokalani*, 14 Hawaii 88 (1902); *In re Boundaries of Paunau*, 24 Hawaii 546 (1918); *Territory* v. *Gay, supra; Bishop* v. *Mahiko,* 35 Hawaii 605 (1940).

17. *Jones* v. *Meek*, 2 Hawaii 9 (1866); *In re Boundaries of Kewalo, supra; In re Boundaries of Paakea,* 5 Hawaii 154 (1884); *Harris* v. *Carter, supra; In re Kakaako, supra*.

Some *konohikis* failed to take advantage of even the second extension of time granted in 1860 and, as a further relief for them, on December 16, 1892,[18] the legislature authorized the minister of interior to issue Royal Patents to all *konohikis* or to their heirs or assigns where such *konohikis* had failed to receive awards for their lands from the Land Commission or from the minister of interior as authorized by the Act of August 24, 1860; "provided, however, that the names of such *konohikis* and of their unawarded lands appear in the Mahele Book of 1848, and where the said lands have not in the meantime been disposed of by the Government, and that the Government shall receive one-third (1/3) of the unimproved value of such lands at the date of such *mahele*."

The Act further provided that these Royal Patents were to be issued on surveys approved by the Surveyor General of the kingdom or upon the certificate of the Commissioner of Boundaries, and that the act "shall not be construed to conflict with or invalidate any grant or land sale made heretofore by the Government or any existing award."

Under the Act, the *konohikis* were allowed until January 1, 1895, to present their claims to the minister of interior, and anyone who failed to file his claim before that date was forever barred and his rights reverted to the government. Nearly all of the *konohikis* who participated in *The Great Mahele* of 1848 or their successors in interest took advantage of this Act and obtained title to their *konohiki* lands.[19]

18. *Laws of Hawaii, 1892; Revised Laws of Hawaii, 1925*, vol. II, p. 2151.

19. The term *konohiki* originally referred to a land agent appointed by a superior chief. However, in time, *konohiki* was extended to include the chief himself. *Territory* v. *Bishop Trust Company, Ltd.*, 41 Hawaii 358 (1956).

4. CROWN AND GOVERNMENT LANDS

Even before the *mahele*, or division, of lands with the high chiefs and lesser *konohikis* was completed, King Kamehameha III planned the further subdivision of his reserved lands between the government and himself. The king was deeply concerned over the hostile activities of the foreigners in the Islands. He did not want his lands to be considered public domain and subject to confiscation by a foreign power in the event of a conquest. And he desired complete and free control over his lands.[1]

Thus, on March 8, 1848, a day after the completion of *The Great Mahele*, Kamehameha III signed and sealed two instruments, also recorded in the Mahele Book. Both instruments were written in Hawaiian and translated into English by the Supreme Court of Hawaii in the case of *In re Matters of Estate of His Majesty Kamehameha IV*.[2]

The first instrument was translated as follows: "Know all men by these presents, that I, Kamehameha III, by the Grace of God, King of these Hawaiian Islands, have given this day of my own free will and have made over and set apart forever to the chiefs and people the larger part of my royal land, for the use and benefit of the Hawaiian Government, therefore by this instrument I hereby retain (or reserve) for myself and for my heirs and successors forever, my lands inscribed at pages 178, 182, 184, 186, 190, 194, 200, 204, 206, 210, 212, 214, 216, 218, 220, 222, of this book, these lands are set apart for me and for my heirs and successors forever, as my own property exclusively."

The other instrument was translated thus: "Know all men by these presents, that I, Kamehameha III, by the Grace of God, King of these Hawaiian Islands, do hereby give, make over and set apart forever to the chiefs and people of my Kingdom, and convey all my rights, title and interest in the lands situated here in the Hawaiian Islands, inscribed on pages 179 to 225, both inclusive, of this book, to have and to hold to my chiefs and people forever."

---

1. *Privy Council Records*, vol. IV, pp. 250-308; *In re Matters of Estate of His Majesty Kamehameha IV*, 2 Hawaii 715 (1864).
2. 2 Hawaii 715 (1864).

By the above two instruments, Kamehameha III divided the lands he had reserved for himself in *The Great Mahele* into two separate parts. The smaller portion he retained for his personal use; the larger portion he gave "to the chiefs and people." That portion retained by Kamehameha III became known as "Crown Lands," and that portion given "to the chiefs and people" became known as "Government Lands."

On June 7, 1848,[3] a grateful legislature enacted a statute confirming Kamehameha III's act of March 8, 1848. The statute read in part:

"Whereas, It hath pleased His Most Gracious Majesty Kamehameha III, the King, after reserving certain lands to himself as his own private property, to surrender and forever make over unto his Chiefs and People, the greater portion of his Royal Domain:

"And Whereas, It hath pleased our Sovereign Lord the King, to place the lands so made over to his Chiefs and People, in the keeping of the House of Nobles and Representatives, or such person or persons, as they may from time to time appoint, to be disposed of in such manner as the House of Nobles and Representatives may direct, and as may best promote the prosperity of this kingdom and the dignity of the Hawaiian Crown: Therefore,

"Be it Enacted by the House of Nobles and Representatives of the Hawaiian Islands, in Legislative Council assembled:

"That, expressing our deepest thanks to His Majesty for this noble and truly royal gift, we do hereby solemnly confirm this great act of our good King, and declare the following named lands, viz: [here follow the names of the lands] To be the private lands of His Majesty Kamehameha III, to have and to hold to himself, his heirs, and successors, forever; and said lands shall be regulated and disposed of according to his royal will and pleasure subject only to the rights of tenants.

"And be it further enacted, That we do hereby in the name of the Chiefs and People of the Hawaiian Islands, accept of the following lands, viz: [here follow the names of the lands] Made over to the Chiefs and People, by our Sov-

3. *Laws of Hawaii, 1848*, p. 22; *Revised Laws of Hawaii, 1925*, vol. II, pp. 2152-2176.

ereign Lord the King, and we do hereby declare those lands to be set apart as the lands of the Hawaiian Government, subject always to the rights of tenants. . . .

"And Be It Further Enacted, That, in accordance with ancient custom, the following lands, viz: [here follow the names of the lands] Shall be and the same are hereby set apart for the use of the Fort in Honolulu to be cultivated by soldiers and other tenants. . . ."

The Crown Lands and the Government Lands included both *ahupuaas* and *ili kuponos*. The list of Crown Lands covered 138 individual names on the Islands of Hawaii, Maui, Molokai, Oahu, and Kauai. In the list of Government Lands were 769 individual names on the Islands of Hawaii, Maui, Molokai, Kahoolawe, Oahu, Kauai, and Niihau. The Fort Lands, which were Government Lands set aside for a specific purpose, consisted only of *ilis*. There were 52 *ilis* set aside for the soldiers on Oahu: 31 *ilis* of Honolulu, 2 *ilis* of Kalihi, and 19 *ilis* of Waikiki, all in the District of Kona, Island of Oahu.

By his surrender of the larger portion of his reserved lands to the government, Kamehameha III disposed of the question of his payment of commutation to the government. And, unlike the chiefs and *konohikis* who had participated in The Mahele of 1848, it was not necessary for Kamehameha III to obtain an award for his lands from the Land Commission. He already had perfect title to his Crown Lands.[4]

Until the passage of the Act of January 3, 1865,[5] which made Crown Lands inalienable, Kamehameha III and his successors did as they pleased with the Crown Lands, selling, leasing, and mortgaging them at will. Upon the overthrow of the monarchy in 1893, the remaining Crown Lands were taken over by the new government and thereafter made part of the public domain.

Following the division of the lands into Crown, Government, and Konohiki Lands, from time to time portions of the Government Lands were sold as a means of obtaining revenue to meet the increasing costs of the Government. Purchasers of these lands were issued documents called "Grants" or "Royal Patent Grants." These differed from

4. *Harris* v. *Carter*, 6 Hawaii 195 (1877).
5. *Laws of Hawaii, 1864*, p. 69; *Revised Laws of Hawaii, 1925*, vol. II, pp. 2177-2179.

No. 1153

ROYAL PATENT.

KAMEHAMEHA III., By the grace of God, King of the Hawaiian Islands, by this His Royal Patent, makes known unto all men, that he has for himself and his successors in office, this day granted and given, absolutely, in Fee Simple unto *E Bailey* his faithful and loyally disposed subject for the consideration of *seven 5/100 dollars,* paid into the Royal Exchequer, all that piece of Land, situated at *Ohia Waikapu* in the Island of *Maui* , and described as follows:

Beginning at the South corner of Pipinui's lot in the creek of Waikapu, and running N. 15° E. 1.22 chains along Pipinui, thence S. 68° E. 1.22 chains, along Mumuku's lot, thence S. 16° W. 1.10 chains along Mumuku's lot, to creek, thence N. 71° W. 1.23 chains along creek to place of beginning.

Reserving the rights of Native Tenants,

Containing *0.74* Acres, more or less: excepting and reserving to the Hawaiian Government, all mineral or metallic Mines of every description.
To have and to hold the above granted Land in Fee Simple, unto the said *E. Bailey* , *his* Heirs and Assigns forever, subject to the taxes to be from time to time imposed by the Legislative Council equally, upon all landed Property held in Fee Simple.

In Witness Whereof, I have hereunto set my Hand, and caused the Great Seal of the Hawaiian Islands to be affixed, at Honolulu, this *eleventh* day of *Oulai* 1853

Signed Kamehameha

Signed Keoni Ana,

the Royal Patents issued upon Land Commission Awards. It was not necessary for the recipients of the Royal Patent Grants to obtain an award for their land from the Land Commission.

5. KULEANA LANDS

The lands identified and separated in 1848 as Crown Lands, Government Lands, and Konohiki Lands were all "subject to the rights of native tenants."[1] As King Kamehameha III, the government, and the various high chiefs and lesser *konohikis* began to sell portions of their lands, many questions arose with reference to the protection of the "rights of native tenants." To clarify the situation, the Privy Council took the matter under consideration on October 19, 1849.[2] After several months of discussion, finally on December 21, 1849, the Privy Council adopted four resolutions introduced at an earlier date by William Lee, as a means of protecting the "rights of native tenants."

These resolutions authorized the Land Commission to award fee simple titles to all native tenants who occupied and improved any portion of Crown, Government, or Konohiki Lands. Except for the houselots located in the districts of Honolulu, Lahaina, and Hilo, these awards were to be free of commutation.

On August 6, 1850,[3] the legislature confirmed the resolutions of the Privy Council, and added certain provisions of its own dealing with the rights of native tenants in lands to which the chiefs and *konohikis* had taken fee simple titles. Although previously, on November 11, 1846,[4] the

---

1. *Laws of Hawaii, 1848*, p. 22; *Revised Laws of Hawaii, 1925*, vol. II, pp. 2152-2176; *Harris* v. *Carter*, 6 Hawaii 195 (1877); *In re Kakaako*, 30 Hawaii 666 (1928).

2. *Privy Council Records*, vol. III, p. 384. The matter was thereafter discussed on November 27, December 12, 20, 21, 1849. *Privy Council Records*, vol. III, pp. 404, 411-412, 415, and 417-419.

3. *Laws of Hawaii, 1850*, p. 202; *Revised Laws of Hawaii, 1925*, vol. II, pp. 2141-2142.

4. *Laws of Hawaii, 1847; Revised Laws of Hawaii, 1925*, vol. II, p. 2193.

legislature had enacted a statute authorizing the native tenants to apply to the minister of interior for the purchase of lands which they had actually cultivated, it was this Act of August 6, 1850, that truly paved the way for the native tenants, the common people, to acquire their own lands.

Before receiving awards for their lands from the Land Commission under this Act of 1850, the native tenants were required to prove that they actually cultivated those lands for a living. They were not permitted to acquire waste lands or lands which they cultivated "with the seeming intention of enlarging their lots." The lands confirmed to the tenants under this Act of 1850 were required to be surveyed before the Land Commission was authorized to issue any award on such lands. These lands, awarded to the native tenants under this Act of 1850, became known as "*kuleana* lands." They are completely independent of the *ahupuaas* or *ili kuponos* within which they are situated.[5]

Except for the houselots in Honolulu, Lahaina, and Hilo, the native tenants were awarded their *kuleanas* free of commutation. The owner of the *ahupuaa* or *ili kupono*, out of which the different *kuleanas* were taken, was deemed responsible for the settlement of the whole government commutation. However, awards for the houselots in Honolulu, Lahaina, and Hilo were subject to commutation, which was set at one fourth of the value of the unimproved land as of the date of the award. These houselots were not in any *ahupuaa* or *ili kupono* whose chief was deemed responsible for the commutation.[6]

Though other lands escheated to the government upon the death of the owner without an heir, the *kuleanas* escheated to the owner of the *ahupuaa* or *ili kupono* within which it was located. Since the owner of the *ahupuaa* or *ili kupono* was responsible for the commutation of the *kuleanas* situated within his *ahupuaa* or *ili kupono*, he was deemed to have the reversionary interest in those *kuleanas*. However, the houselots in Honolulu, Lahaina, and Hilo escheated to the government.[7]

5. *Akowai* v. *Lupong,* 4 Hawaii 259 (1880); *Judd* v. *Kuanalewa,* 6 Hawaii 329 (1882).

6. *Keeliokalani* v. *Robinson,* 2 Hawaii 522 (1860); *Kanaina* v. *Long,* 3 Hawaii 335 (1872); *Harris* v. *Carter,* 6 Hawaii 195 (1877); *Minister of Interior* v. *Papaikou Sugar Co.,* 8 Hawaii 125 (1890).

7. *Kahoomana* v. *Moehonua,* 3 Hawaii 635 (1875).

Until its dissolution on March 31, 1855, the Land Commission issued thousands of awards to the native tenants for their *kuleanas*. However, there were many native tenants who failed to receive awards for the lands they had occupied and improved. Some failed to file their claims with the Land Commission and others, after filing their claims, failed to appear before the Land Commission to support their claims. Many in the latter group, after filing their claims, relinquished such claims to the chiefs of the *ahupuaas* or *ili kuponos* in which their cultivated lands were situated.

Whereas over 1,500,000 acres of land were set aside for the chiefs in *The Great Mahele* of 1848, and approximately 1,000,000 acres were reserved by Kamehameha III as "Crown Lands," and 1,500,000 acres were given by the king to the "government and people," less than 30,000 acres of land were awarded to the native tenants. However, these tracts of land awarded to the native tenants consisted chiefly of taro lands and were considered the more valuable lands in the Islands.[8] The awarding of these *kuleanas* to the native tenants completed the *mahele*, or division, of the lands within the Islands into Crown Lands, Government Lands, Konohiki Lands, and Kuleana Lands, and brought to an end the ancient system of land tenure in the Hawaiian Kingdom.[9]

8. Ralph S. Kuykendall, *The Hawaiian Kingdom, 1778-1854* (Honolulu: University of Hawaii, 1938). The Mahele Book, Office of the Commissioner of Public Lands, Territorial Office Building, Honolulu, Territory of Hawaii.

9. Copies of the Land Commission Awards, the Royal Patents issued on those awards, together with the other grants from the various governments of the Hawaiian Islands, are filed in the Office of the Commissioner of Public Lands, Territorial Office Building, Honolulu, Territory of Hawaii.

BIBLIOGRAPHY

Kuykendall, Ralph S., *The Hawaiian Kingdom: Foundation and Transformation, 1778-1854.* Honolulu: University of Hawaii, 1938.

Thurston, Lorrin A., *The Fundamental Law of Hawaii.* Honolulu: The Hawaiian Gazette Company, Ltd., 1904.

The Mahele Book. In the office of the Commissioner of Public Lands, Territorial Office Building, Honolulu.

Journals of the Legislature, October, 1846. In the Public Archives of Hawaii, Honolulu.

Privy Council Records. In the Public Archives of Hawaii, Honolulu.

Statutes of the Kingdom and of the Territory of Hawaii:
  Laws of Hawaii: 1846, 1847, 1848, 1850, 1852, 1854, 1860, 1862, 1864, 1892, 1909.
  Revised Laws of Hawaii, 1925, Vol. II, pp. 2120-2236, *Principles Adopted By The Board of Commissioners To Quiet Land Titles.*

Hawaiian Cases, Supreme Court of Hawaii:
  Akowai v. *Lupong,* 4 Hawaii 259 (1880)
  Atcherly v. *Lewers & Cooke,* 18 Hawaii 639 (1908)
  Bishop v. *Kalua,* 36 Hawaii 164 (1942)
  Bishop v. *Mahiko,* 35 Hawaii 608 (1940)
  Bishop v. *Namakaala & Kahinukawa,* 2 Hawaii 238 (1860)
  Board of Education v. *Bailey,* 3 Hawaii 702 (1876)
  Boundaries of Kapoino, 8 Hawaii 1 (1889)
  Brunz v. *Minister of Interior,* 3 Hawaii 783 (1877)
  Cornwell v. *Board of Education,* 4 Hawaii 540 (1882)
  Davis v. *Brewer,* 3 Hawaii 270 (1871)
  Dowsett v. *Maukeala,* 10 Hawaii 166 (1895)
  Greenwell v. *Paris,* 6 Hawaii 315 (1882)
  Harris v. *Carter,* 6 Hawaii 195 (1877)
  Horner v. *Kumuliilii,* 10 Hawaii 174 (1895)
  In re Austin (*Land Title, Waimalu*), 33 Hawaii 832 (1936)
  In re Boundaries of Kapoino, 8 Hawaii 1 (1889)
  In re Boundaries of Kewalo, 3 Hawaii 9 (1866)
  In re Boundaries of Paunau, 24 Hawaii 546 (1918)

In re Boundaries of Pulehunui, 4 Hawaii 239 (1879)
In re Kakaako, 30 Hawaii 666 (1928)
In re Matters of Estate of His Majesty Kamehameha IV, 2 Hawaii 715 (1864)
In re Title of Kioloku, 25 Hawaii 357 (1920)
In re Title of Pa Pelekane, 21 Hawaii 175 (1912)
Jones v. *Meek*, 2 Hawaii 9 (1857)
Judd v. *Kuanalewa*, 6 Hawaii 329 (1882)
Kaai v. *Mahuka*, 5 Hawaii 354 (1885)
Kahoomana v. *Minister of Interior*, 3 Hawaii 635 (1875)
Kalama v. *Kekuanoa & Ii*, 2 Hawaii 202 (1857)
Kanaina v. *Long*, 3 Hawaii 335 (1872)
Kapiolani Estate v. *Atcherly*, 21 Hawaii 441 (1912)
Keelikolani v. *Robinson*, 2 Hawaii 436, 522 (1862)
Kekiekie v. *Dennis*, 1 Hawaii 69 (1851)
Kenoa v. *Meek*, 6 Hawaii 63 (1871)
Knudsen v. *Board of Education*, 8 Hawaii 60 (1890)
Kukiiahu v. *Mahuka*, 5 Hawaii 354 (1885)
Laanui v. *Puohu*, 2 Hawaii 161 (1859)
Minister of Interior v. *Papaikou Sugar Company*, 8 Hawaii 125 (1890)
Mist v. *Kawelo*, 11 Hawaii 587 (1898)
Oni v. *Meek*, 2 Hawaii 87 (1858)
Pedro v. *Chun Yun Fan*, 4 Hawaii 461 (1882)
Rose v. *Yoshimura*, 11 Hawaii 30 (1897)
Shipman v. *Nawahi*, 5 Hawaii 571 (1886)
Territory v. *Bishop Trust Company, Ltd.*, Supreme Court Number 3005 (1956)
Territory v. *Gay*, 26 Hawaii 382 (1922)
Territory v. *Gay*, 31 Hawaii 376 (1930)
Territory v. *Liliuokalani*, 14 Hawaii 88 (1902)
Thurston v. *Bishop*, 7 Hawaii 421, 438 (1888)

Hawaiian Cases, United States Supreme Court:
Atcherly v. *Lewers & Cooke*, 222 United States 285 (1911)
Kapiolani Estate v. *Atcherly*, 238 United States 119 (1915)

Hawaiian Cases, Federal Circuit of Appeals:
Territory v. *Hutchinson Sugar Plantation Company*, 272 Federal 856 (C.C.A. 9th 1921)